Woman

OF

God

"FROM NOWHERE TO EVERYWHERE!"

Apostle Lee Harris

DEDICATION

To my love, Davida King-Harris, who is the greatest
Woman of God I've ever met. Her grace and kindness
have been a source of amazement as she operates in this
life as a Wife, Mother, Grandmother, Daughter, and
Minister of the Gospel. Her love and words of
encouragement impact the lives of everyone who meets
her. God has truly taken her "From Nowhere to
Everywhere".

ACKNOWLEDGMENTS

Many thanks to **Walking Into Your Destiny, LLC** for allowing me the opportunity to publish this book.

MESSAGE TO THE DAUGHTERS OF GOD...

Woman of God, the time has come for you to operate in the full capacity of your mind. God, in His sovereignty (having supreme power), has given you the power and mindset to come out from the control of others—to stand and declare that the day God has promised to elevate you to the forefront of living has arrived. The thoughts of others will intimidate you no longer because this global vision is from God. 'From Nowhere to Everywhere' is now your state of mind.

God has more for you than the neighborhood mentality of going to the store, church, and back home. Your eyes have yet to see the glorious things He has in store for you! So, arise from the low self-esteem thinking to the powerhouse that you are. See yourself being the dream that's in you—free from the limitations and restraints you've allowed in your life. Walk in the confidence that comes from God. It's time to make your mark on the world. I'll see you at the Top where you belong!

Apostle Lee Harris

PART I

"FROM NOWHERE TO EVERYWHERE"

WOMAN OF GOD "BECAUSE"

In 1ˢᵗ Corinthians 15:9-10 (NKJV), Paul stated, **"For I am the least of the Apostles, who am not worthy to be called an Apostle, because I persecuted the church of God."** Woman of God, what is the *because* that has happened in your past you haven't quite gotten over yet? What things have made you feel like you could never rise above the label, the negative self-image, and the shame of those things? God has sent me to tell you that *who* you were did not stop Him from choosing you to become *what* you are in Him.

Paul says in the next verse, **"But by the grace of God I am what I am, and His grace toward me was not in vain; but I labored more abundantly than they all, yet not I, but the grace of God which was with me."**

Woman of God, your past *because* has nothing to do with *what* God has formed and called you to be. It is by His grace and His grace alone that you can, by laboring in His grace, rise and become all He has graced you to become before you had any negative *because* in your life.

Don't let what He has already done in you be in vain. Remove the *because* so the *what* you are will become manifested in your life. No more low self-confidence, no more saying *if I hadn't done that* or *I should have known better*. Let it go. You are still here; get up and become everything God has ordained you to become by His marvelous Grace. Whatever *because* that comes to mind, let it go; it no longer has any power over you. You are worthy of what God has called you, so work with

His Grace. I'll see you at the Top where you belong!

WOMAN OF GOD "CONDITION CHANGED"

Acts 3:2-3 (NKJV) tells a story of a lame man. It states, **"And a certain man lame from his mother's womb was carried, whom they laid daily at the gate of the temple which is called Beautiful, to ask alms from those who entered the temple; who, seeing Peter and John about to go into the temple, asked for alms."** In this passage, we find a man crippled or lamed from his mother's womb. That was his *condition* that caused him to beg for support.

Woman of God, what has brought lameness into your life? What has crippled you financially, emotionally, and spiritually? Was it from a divorce, an addiction, loss of a loved one, sickness, disease, out of work, incarceration, low self-esteem, or depression? All are a condition from something.

No matter what your condition is, God wants to change your condition through the power that comes through faith in the name of Jesus. Once He changes your condition, then you'll change your way of supporting yourself. Rise from that condition by the power of His name into His perfect soundness. I'll meet you at the Top where you belong!

WOMAN OF GOD "HOPE AGAINST HOPE"

When the fire is out of your hope and when all hope seems gone, it's important that you know you have come to the place in your life where you're at a place called *hope against hope*. It is in this place that miracles happen for you. This is the place where you realize that God is your only source. It's not the doctors, the bank, the landlord, your spouse, or the government—no one is your source but God Himself.

The Creator of all things will move in your life as He did for Abraham who hoped against hope. Abraham believed; therefore, he became what God had promised him. Woman of God, it may not look like it, but against hope IN hope, you are going to the Top where you belong in this life—on this side of Heaven. God bless you always. Amen

WOMAN OF GOD "THE WEIGHT IS FALLING"

I am so proud of you for all the weight you have lost over the few months you have started your walk to the Top! Wow! The weight of low self-esteem, GONE! The weight of needing approval by others, GONE! Being tossed back and forth by the opinions of people, GONE! Worrying over things you can't change, GONE! Asking yourself why *they* won't accept you, GONE!

I know you feel better because you certainly look better! The weight is falling, and there is no turning back! Look at your spiritual muscles! Your persistence and resistance are paying off for you!

You are so much stronger today than you were yesterday! Don't give up now! The Top has need of You! By the way, I will see you at the Top where you belong!

WOMAN OF GOD "SEEK GOD'S TRUTH"

Truth will get rid of facts. Your life is full of facts, but God's Word is full of truth to rid your life of the facts. Believe His Word, speak His Word, and abide by His Word and you'll see the facts removed and the truth will become manifested. The truth is, you *are* what God says you are, you can *do* what God says you can do, and you can *have* whatever He says you can have. Now that's the Truth! Believe it, receive it, and own it. You are a blessing in Jesus' name. Amen.

WOMAN OF GOD "YOU GOT THIS"

When you made the choice of choosing life, you made the choice of choosing all that life brings, which means you must stand strong even when you don't think you can. This is not wasted time you're going through right now. There's a strength within you which you haven't tapped into yet. But once you pull on it, you will be amazed at how wonderfully God has designed you and equipped you with His glory causing you to enter a realm of power and authority that will catapult you to a next level of purpose. This next level will have you worshipping God for His grace, mercy, and peace like you never have before. This right here, you got this right here!

WOMAN OF GOD "STAND UP IN YOUR AUTHORITY"

Do you believe God has your best interest at heart? I'm not speaking of wishful thinking. Do you believe He knows of your now and your tomorrow? Well, if you *really* believe, rest in His attributes, His grace, His mercy, and His peace. Walk in full confidence that God is working on your behalf always. You have the authority from Almighty God to move in the anointing that's on your life. You have confidence in knowing He won't leave you nor forsake you—ever. He has you, and He needs you. I see you headed to the Top where you belong!

WOMAN OF GOD "THERE IS GLORY IN THIS"

There's a depth in you with much hidden treasures to be excavated. The enemy wants you to think there's no purpose to the negatives that are taking place in your life, but God is removing the waste while unloading what's disguised as genuine but is really fake.

Your true treasures are being unearthed during this process of pain. Stay hopeful and anchored in hope. For you will see the glory of the Lord shine in your life to a dimension that will carry you where you never dreamed of going. I'll see you at the Top where you belong!

WOMAN OF GOD "DISCOURAGED, BUT STILL ANOINTED"

You may find yourself discouraged today, but know you're still anointed. God has appointed His natural to be on your natural causing you to be SUPERNATURAL. Things may not be going your way, but you're still anointed. You may have lost your employment, but you're still anointed. You may feel betrayed, but you're still anointed. You may experience financial lack, but you're still anointed. There may be mountains in your path, but you're still anointed. There may be a disruption to your family structure, but you're still anointed. You may have sickness and pain in your body, but you're still anointed. You may be addicted to alcohol, drugs, or pornography, but you're still anointed.

Because you're anointed, God will destroy every yoke off you. I loose the anointing of 'more than enough' over your life by the authority of words of faith through the power of the Holy Spirit within me. You're now free to move in the liberating power of God through Jesus Christ, of whom the Son sets free is free indeed. So be it... I'll see you at the Top where you belong!

WOMAN OF GOD "YOU'RE HONORABLE IN THE SIGHT OF GOD"

You've made mistakes, you've taken wrong turns, you've even stepped out of bounds more than a few times, but you're still honorable in the sight of Him who calls you as He sees you. Honorable is the position in which He has called you. He has graced you with forgiveness and favor. You have not worked for, nor earned this grace of yourself. Your actions will soon line up with your God-placed position of being *honorable*.

Cast off the cloaks of defeat, disappointment, and despair. No longer ask yourself: *How could I have?* Instead, slip back into the garment of praise and your position of being *honorable*. Your heart will love you for it. Your God always has! I will see you at the Top where the *honorable* you belong.

WOMAN OF GOD "TAKE OFF THAT GOWN OF REJECTION"

What was once a beautiful thing to wear now only reminds you of hurt and pain. How can you not see the rainbow of many colors for your life—a vibrant gown full of energy and enthusiasm for you to wear? Stop looking into the mirror of rejection and pick up the mirror that God has that will show you as the apple of His eye—beautifully and wonderfully made. You can do all things through Christ who strengthens you. You got this! I'll see you at the Top where you belong!

WOMAN OF GOD "YOU ARE A DIAMOND"

Some say that diamonds are a girl's best friend. Natural diamonds are formed at high-pressure, high-temperature conditions. That best describes your life right now. Woman of God, the pressures and temperatures you are experiencing are making you into a glowing masterpiece of God's brilliance that will soon become your testimony of His goodness.

WOMAN OF GOD "THE BATTLE IS FOR YOUR MIND"

The enemy knows if he can get your mind, he has you. That's why your mind is the grand prize. He'll keep you depressed, fearful, in despair, desperate, cunning, hopeless, betrayed, ashamed, and condemned. But you still have access to the power of the Holy Spirit, who will arrange your life to straighten out the path that God has ordained for you. Your access comes by making up in your mind what you want and trusting Him by faith and not by feelings or past outcomes, nor sights.

You have the strength to abide under His wings of protection by deciding to cross over in your mind. Trust in the LORD and in the power of His might and lean not on your own understanding. Switch now, woman of God, by faith, and I assure you God will take you in Him where you couldn't even dream of going. Take this Word of Impact, act on it, and allow it to dominate your mind to transform your life. Have faith in God!

WOMAN OF GOD "IGNORE THE BAFFLING WINDS"

Don't allow the baffling winds of others, doubts, fears, rejection, and uncertainties to keep you from reaching forward and taking hold of the promises of God for your life. The enemy sends those baffling winds to make you go backwards— back to low self-esteem, unwise relationships, cheating, stealing, lying, anger, drinking, drugs, cursing, worry, and the likes. But God, who gives strength to those who, by faith, reach through the baffling winds, will protect you from the elements and see that your life will be one of extraordinary exploits to His Glory. Peace be still! I will see you at the Top!

WOMAN OF GOD "BY FAITH"

By faith, Sarah (herself) received strength to conceive seed because she judged Him faithful who had promised. When people around you are telling you what you believe God for will not happen, especially if you have been waiting for some time now and the promise hasn't happened, do what Sarah did: By faith, HERSELF received strength!

You, YOURSELF, receive God's strength through FAITH until His promises happen in your life! Take charge of your relationship with the promises of God, YOURSELF, by faith! I will see you at the Top!

WOMAN OF GOD "RECEIVE PERFECT SOUNDNESS"

There was a lame man in Acts 3 of the Holy Bible crippled *from* his mother's womb and who never walked, but by faith, he was healed. I hear the LORD saying to you that the situations, circumstances, and issues that has you crippled, through faith in His name, you, have perfect soundness and now you can jump, leap, walk, and rejoice because nothing can keep you from living and moving in Him! Do not fear... Do not fear... Do not fear! Perfect soundness is yours! So, jump, leap, and praise your way to the Top!

WOMAN OF GOD "LIVE A LIFE OF MEANING"

I once heard someone say, "The meaning of life is a life of meaning." What is the meaning of your life? What is the passion that drives you? What makes your life count? The meaning of your life is God's purpose for your life—what you were born to do.

Having a passion for doing the thing you were born to do is what drives you. And what makes your life count is when you live to make a positive difference in the lives of others. Know *who* you are, then be *who* you know, so you can say, "I am who I am by the Grace of God; therefore, I labor more abundantly." I will see you at the Top where you belong!

WOMAN OF GOD "RECEIVE HIS GRACE"

He gave his grace to you that you may become more than ordinary—that you may become extraordinary. By His grace, He wants you to spend your life by investing into people and not waste your life on those who only want to use, hurt, and control you. He has gifted you for His glory and made life available to you that you may have life more abundantly through His Son, Jesus Christ. Is there anything too hard for the LORD? If your answer is no, then act like you KNOW from this moment forward! Extraordinary is within your reach, and its desire is for you. I will see you at the Top!

WOMAN OF GOD "GO FOR IT"

Sometimes, all we need is someone to believe in us and what we are doing to help make our lives' work for us. We need someone who can see us at a level that maybe we can't see ourselves at yet while we pursue that thing which God has called us to do.

Woman of God, I can see you at that level, and so can God! So, start that ministry, get that degree, start that career/business, apply for that promotion/job, buy that car/house, take that Vacation, etc. Whatever that thing is, make sure you have a mountaintop experience! And by the way, I will see you there!

WOMAN OF GOD "IN SPITE OF"

It won't/can't outlast you and your faith in the name of Jesus through faith in His name. Don't believe the uncertainties, negative situations, lies of the enemy, emotional lows, impoverished thoughts, and suicidal thoughts. They can't outlast you because He has granted you a great force that will cause you to stand—PATIENCE.

The Greek word for patience is 'HUPOMONE', meaning cheerful, endurance and consistency. Woman of God, you have 'in spite of's' on the inside of you! In spite of how it looks, how you feel, what they say, what they do, and what they don't do—you have some 'in spite of's' and your God will exalt you in due time! I see where you are headed—to the Top!

WOMAN OF GOD "I AM WITH YOU"

Thus, says the Lord, "I am with you in this season. You will not feel alone because you will *know* that you are not alone! You will not feel depressed in this season because of the great expectations that are just ahead of you! You will not feel any pressure to *be* or *do* because My Spirit will lead you and direct your path! In this season, you will enjoy Me as I provide for you." Have faith in God!

WOMAN OF GOD "SHED YOUR TEARS"

Your tears are now tears of cleansing. The difference is your mindset—a mind of trust and not fear. Tears of joy, expectation, healing, provision, peace, forgiveness, His unconditional love, and your bright future will begin to flow. So, yes, let the tears flow as the Spirit of the LORD springs forth a new level of life in you! I will see you at the Top where you belong!

WOMAN OF GOD "DETERMINE TO LIVE"

It's not your performance but your flowing in the Spirit of God. God makes you to soar above circumstances, trials, and temptations because you dwell in the power of an endless life that Jesus provides for you. It's time for you to arise and let God take you where He wants to take you according to the power of an endless life. Have faith in God!

<u>WOMAN OF GOD "YOU ARE BEAUTIFUL"</u>

Your physical beauty, at its best, is subjective. Your real beauty reflects the loving attitude you wear when you don't have the resources to go to the hairdresser or can't afford the latest name brand attire. Yet, you wear *you* well because what you wear is a priceless attitude of beauty.

Oh, I see you wearing that grateful attitude of thanksgiving for having come through the storms of life, yet still in your right mind when those around you thought they were seeing the last of you. Little did they know you were gearing up to shine brighter than ever!

Because of your continuing faith in God, it was only a matter of time before what was on the inside of you would radiate on the outside of you! Yes, that's the beautiful you—the apple of your Heavenly Father's eye. I hear the Lord saying, "The glory of the LORD is upon you, and because of your inner beauty of faith, shut doors will now swing wide open for you, and plenty will be yours!" There is a winner in you, so just win, Lady! I'll see you at the Top where you belong!

WOMAN OF GOD "THE HARVEST IS YOURS"

There are acres in your mind that need developing so you can have a healthy harvest where the enemy would like for those acres to lie in waste due to loss, heartache, low self- esteem, broken relationships, unfulfilled dreams, and hopelessness. God will give you wisdom to develop your mind by renewing your mind so that your mind will work for you. The Lord said to Abraham in Genesis 13:14-15 (NKJV), **"Lift your eyes now and look from the place where you are—northward, southward, eastward, and westward; for all the land which you see I give to you and your descendants**

forever." Woman of God, enjoy the harvest, and I will see you at the Top where you belong!

WOMAN OF GOD "HE HAS YOU"

After her brief visit with Jesus, the Samaritan woman said to the people in her city, **"Come, see a Man who told me all things that I ever did. Could this be the Christ?"** (John 4:29 NKJV) This woman had five husbands to leave her, and the man she was living with didn't see her as a wife. She felt so happy to know that this man (the Christ) at the well knew everything she had ever did—every tear she had cried, every rejection, every thought of suicide, every doubt of worthiness, every act of self-medication—everything she had ever done.

Could this be the Christ? Yes, and He's the same Christ who is there for your sleepless nights, pains, tears, needs, and confusions. He is the certainty in your uncertainties. He knows what He's going to do in you, through you, and for you! Woman of God, He has you! Believe that He has you!!! I will see you at the Top where you belong!

WOMAN OF GOD "YOU ARE STRONG"

You keep saying you are a strong woman, but you're not making strong woman decisions. What you do and say must line up for your life to work *for* you and not *against* you. You can trust God with your heart and mind—doing what's right no matter how you feel. Obey God and leave the consequences of your obedience up to Him who you can trust with the outcome. Never stop your confession that you are a strong woman of God and continue to do what strong women do. You're headed to the Top where you belong!

WOMAN OF GOD "COME TO YOURSELF"

The enemy has tried to make you feel as though you have a mental illness problem, but God has kept His hand on your mind, so you would not lose your mind to the threats of the enemy. Woman of God, you are not mentally ill; you are mentally tired. Hence, you have been operating and making decisions from a mentally tired mind. But that hasn't been working out for you.

How can you choose a mate when you are mentally tired? How can you raise your family when you are mentally tired? You keep finding yourself in situations because you are mentally tired. And it's impossible to believe God in a mentally tired state of mind.

You've been in the hog pen of life as you struggle with being mentally tired. But now it's time to come to yourself—back to the mind God has held from the wiles of the enemy's destruction. When you come to yourself, you will get up from where you are and turn toward the life God wants for you in Him. His best is what He wants for you! Come to yourself right now in Jesus name. Perfect soundness of mind is yours! You will head to the Top where you belong!

WOMAN OF GOD "GET IN TOUCH WITH YOURSELF"

When your emotions are all over the place, you must 'get in touch with yourself' by reminding yourself of the core values that make you uniquely you. When the world around you seems to fall apart, you have an inner strength that's your anchor to keep you upright—things that keep you grounded that you love to do that shows who you are—this makes you alive.

I often must go back to the purpose I was born—the big picture of spreading the gospel of Jesus Christ around the world. Get in touch with yourself on this day, so you can stop being taken advantage of or high-jacked by your own feelings.

There's not one person in this world that is better than you at being uniquely you. I'll see you at the Top where you belong!

WOMAN OF GOD "HIDE IN ME"

I hear the Lord saying to you, "I want you so hidden in Me that nothing can shake your faith. No, not one thing can cause you to fear anyone or any circumstances because you have My anointing! After you find rest in Me, you are equipped to speak to any obstacles that may stand in your way of being and doing all I have purposed you to be and do! It's time for you to make your life work through Me." You are Headed to the Top!

WOMAN OF GOD "YOU HAVE THE KEY OF DAVID"

The key of David is upon you, and God will open doors that no one will shut, and He will shut doors that no one will open. Your key is God given authority, so use it! Turn the key. Shut out confusion, dead-end thinking, powerless living, and the likes. Lock that door shut! Now, turn the key to open wisdom from on high, a sound mind, unlimited possibilities, and wholeness. Open doors that will take you to the Top!

WOMAN OF GOD "PRAISE HIM"

Your praise to the LORD is despite anything you're going through! If you can muster up enough willpower to praise Him in the most difficult times of your life, He will hear you and move upon your life in the most incredible ways—far above that which you have envisioned! Oh, I hear a sound coming from you towards Him, and I see Him standing to receive your praise as His Angels prepare to deliver to you what He has promised you! To the Top you go!

WOMAN OF GOD "YOU ARE YOU"

What a 'YOU' you are! With the millions of thoughts that race through your mind all day, you can still fix a thought on Him that connects you to Him—your source that carries you from glory to glory! What a 'YOU' that falls but gets back up! What a 'YOU' left for dead but is still alive— dreaming and moving ahead! What a 'YOU' when talked about, you still smile in between the tears. It is 'YOU' who I see at the Top!

WOMAN OF GOD "DREAM"

Dream today, while you are awake! Dream of your better tomorrow being today. Dream of being healthy, successful, at peace, nothing broken, and nothing missing. Dream of the God-given relationship while using your gifts with passion and drive. Just keep dreaming. Then, you will wake up and live your dreams! God is a Dream Maker! See you at the Top!

WOMAN OF GOD "THE DEVIL IS A LIAR"

Your tears of a future left behind has been a scene of deception the enemy has placed in your mind causing you to think your best days are behind you. He has caused you to think you've blown it because you didn't do all you knew to do with your life this past year. He's twisted your short comings into you coming up short in your mind.

The devil is a liar, and the truth is not in him. Get ready for the finest year of your life! You will please the Lord by faith as you've never pleased Him before! You are a Woman of God. Nothing less than that will be enough to live by faith. Your position is fixed through the finished work of Christ Jesus. Go after it! You serve an amazing God who wants to do amazing things in and through you! I will see you at the Top where you belong!

WOMAN OF GOD "SPRING FORTH"

As a seed hides in a dark, isolated place with its potential inside, and depends on someone above it to water and fertilize it until it springs forth from its hard surroundings, so are you hidden in a somewhat dark, isolated place full of the potential that is in you by your Creator and Maker. The Lord is dependable to both water and fertilize you for your springing forth, bearing much fruit in the light of what He's called you to be.

You are not alone. God hasn't forgotten you. Your star will shine bright in a moment of suddenly. With your fruit ripe, you'll soon be on your way. You are being stabilized in the isolation you're in right now, but you're not alone. The Spirit of the

Lord is at hand to water and fertilize you for your big moments of life! How long? Not long! Relax, and let God finish His great work in you. His best will meet you. Just don't give up!

WOMAN OF GOD "HIS GRACE IS ENOUGH"

Why do you lay awake worrying when you believe God is all knowing and all powerful? Could it be because you have made mistakes that you think maybe God won't move on your behalf? The Spirit of the Lord wants to put you at ease! His grace is enough for you to stop worrying and being in a 'shame' frame of mind and believe Him unto manifestation of what you believe Him for! You can relax because He knows what He will do on your behalf.

WOMAN OF GOD "YOU'RE IN THE RIGHT PLACE"

You're at that place where you don't know what to do. But you're at the right place to see your God like never before! Fear not, stand still, and see the salvation of the Lord. The word 'still' means to present yourself. When you are still, you present yourself before the Lord and see (literally or figuratively) His salvation (deliverance; hence aid, victory, prosperity).

So not knowing what to do is perfect for seeing your God do mighty things in your life when you dare to *fear not* and *stand still* by presenting yourself before Him as an act of worship and *seeing* (literally or with spiritual imagination) the salvation (the things you couldn't figure out or didn't know how to make it work out) of the Lord. This is your day to *stand* and *see*. Oh, He's going to open it up big for you because you dare to trust in Him! You will see this problem no more! Just Win, Lady!

WOMAN OF GOD "IT'S YOUR SEASON"

Ecclesiastes 3:1 (NKJV) states, **"To everything there is a season, a time for every purpose under Heaven."** You have been in a season of lack, fear, tears, pain, hurts, confusion, disappointment, despair, illness, thoughts of suicide, addiction, and failure. But to *everything* there is a season, and that season is NOW OVER! You're moving into a new season and time in your life!

I hear the Lord saying, "You are in a season of renewed hope, vision, prosperity, health, joy, peace, love, courage, works, favor, wisdom, godly decisions, increase, forgiveness, elevation, ministry, relationships, faithfulness, strategies, and miracles." Woman of God, what you want to do, now is the

TIME to make it happen. Your faith will make it happen! Just Win, Lady!

WOMAN OF GOD "PEACE IS YOURS"

You will not let depression get you this time of the year! You are armed and don't have the time for depression! Your circumstance may be like last years, but you're not. You don't have to take part in that realm of emotions anymore. You're coming to show up front and center this season, knowing you're not alone. You have the Holy Spirit living and moving in and through you for harmony. Harmony of peace is yours this season. No pressures and no worries—just relax in Him so He can lead you through to the other side of this season whole.

WOMAN OF GOD "KNOW WHERE YOU STAND"

You should read your feelings as one reads a barometer—an instrument measuring atmospheric pressure used in forecasting the weather and determining altitude. Know where you stand as it regards to your feelings. Sometimes its measure reads: *'SLOW DOWN'*, *'DEAD END AHEAD'*, *'DON'T FALL FOR THAT'*, *'LET IT GO'*, *'DANGER ZONE'*, *'WORTH IT'*, *'WHY?'*, *'NOT GOOD FOR YOU'*, *'YOU KNOW THAT'S NOT TRUE'*, *'DON'T BELONG TO YOU'*, and *'WILL NEVER BE YOURS'*.

Woman of God, remember to be honest in *forecasting* the weather and *determining* altitude. Can you soar with the wrong feelings while doing what's wrong for you? It may feel good, but it may not be good for you. I've been there, done that. I will see you at the Top where you belong!

WOMAN OF GOD "NEVER GIVE UP"

If you don't give up on yourself, chances are you will overcome this latest setback. Give God something to work with, and that something is *you*. Never give up on yourself because when all else fails, you've got to be there for you. A boxer can't win the fight if she must fight in the corner. God is in your corner to refresh you to win. I see your victory at hand!

WOMAN OF GOD "GIVE THANKS"

Giving thanks is an act of your heart that makes you aware that you can give thanks. When giving thanks, the colors of your attitude change from gray to blue, from dull to pastels. Your spirit lifts off to new heights of expectations; therefore, your determination won't short circuit. Thus, turning your thanks into giving you and yours a better you! Thank your way into a better you. You've been down too long; the expiration date on the old you have expired. I see new hair, nails, eyes, and a bright new attitude! I'm thanking God for you right now!

WOMAN OF GOD "YOU LOOK GREAT!"

Look at you! I can't believe your age! you still look showroom new! The grace of God has certainly been all right by you! With all you've gone through and are still facing, you continue to shine with the glory of the Lord upon you. It's amazing how you go about your days, weeks, months, and years still loving, smiling, joyful, peaceful, prayerful, and so graceful.

The broken pieces are being replaced with the new thing He has promised you! And every little thing will be all right. There will be food on your table, and your bills will be paid. You will feel like you've never felt before, so much so you won't remember the shame or sting of the past disappointments. Paradise on earth is what's coming your way!

WOMAN OF GOD "YOUR BEST DAYS ARE AHEAD OF YOU"

Your future is not behind you, but it's in front of you. Your best days have not come and gone, but they are ahead of you. Forget those things behind you—those things keeping you from focusing on the great things that are ahead. No longer have your mind divided between what *was*; give your thinking and focus to what *is* becoming. As day follows night, goodness and mercy shall follow you. Expect to overcome obstacles that once hindered you. May the Lord say of you in this coming year: **Your faith has done this for you**. This is your year for pleasing the Lord!

WOMAN OF GOD "GO ANYWAY"

When you don't want to go on any longer, go on anyway because there is still a spark in you. It may be small, but it's all that's needed to ignite the flame that will start the fire. This fire will carry you into the new direction of thinking, which will change your life. There's still a spark in you—a flame ready to turn into a fire. Smile! You're about to be on FIRE! I'll see you at the Top!

WOMAN OF GOD "IT'S A PROCESS OF TIME"

You're in a process of time, and yesterday's process got you to today's process. You may have failed yesterday, but God passed you into today. Hope for your greater tomorrow is what will bring you through this day. God has you in the making, and in this process, He will leave you plenty of time to enjoy what's left. Don't give up during the process because God is in control! You have an appointment at the Top!

WOMAN OF GOD "THERE'S A MIRACLE WAITING"

Sometimes God will lead you to a situational place that is uncomfortable. While in that place, His words to you are contrary to your logic of thinking but is never in violation to His written word. Because His thoughts are higher than ours, His ways are not logic to our ways of thinking — they are higher. He knows there's a reward in your inner being of obedience to His Word that you could never have without being led into this situational place.

There's a miracle that is awaiting on your obedience in that uncomfortable place. What sense does it make to fill up six water pots with water when wine was the need? But whatever He says, do it. Just do it! I know it makes little sense to you, but do it, anyway! When we humble ourselves under the Words of God, He will do what you could never do—the IMPOSSIBLE. I will see you at the Top where you belong!

WOMAN OF GOD "GET OUT OF THE BOX"

Are you ready to get out of the box—out from the place of small thinking from the limitations of sight? God has divine connections waiting for you. You're the blessing that many need, so get out of the box and spread your wings. You will soon see that you can fly. So, fly above all that has kept you grounded all this time because you have an appointment with success. Teams of people are waiting for your ideas, your dreams, your anointing, your leadership, your books, and your presence.

WOMAN OF GOD "YOU ARE ABLE"

Give yourself flowers even if it's just one stem showing a new appreciation for you. You've had to fight to get by but getting by you're doing. You've had to war when you had nobody by your side, but God has upheld you, so you would know it was just you and He that has gotten you this far. Now, you're ready to explode into your new beginning where you will always be good to yourself.

Don't let your mirror lie to you. You are well able and more than enough. Look yourself in the eyes and say, "With God, I'm well able to lead, to go after, to achieve, to succeed, to excel, to build, make my dreams come true, travel to far-away places—alone, if need be — to be healed, set free, delivered, and whatever else I choose." Woman of God, you are *well* able!

WOMAN OF GOD "YOU ARE DOING A GOOD WORK FOR ME"

In Matthew 26:10-12 (NKJV), Jesus said to the disciples, **"Why do you trouble the woman? For she has done a good work for Me... For in pouring this fragrant oil on My body, she did it for My burial..."**

Woman of God, it please Jesus with the work you are doing for His body. He called what you are doing 'a good work for Me'. Your anointed work is a fragrant oil of the Holy Spirit given to you by the grace of God. Don't allow what others say against the work you are doing in the body of Christ to trouble you any longer. The anointing on your life speaks for itself. So, let the oil flow! Amen.

WOMAN OF GOD "I HAVE APPOINTED YOU"

Jeremiah 1:5 (NKJV) states, **"Before I formed you in the womb I knew you..."** God knew you before the mistakes, the pain, the disappointments, and the losses. Yet, He still appointed you for Himself! If He kept you before, he will keep and get you through these difficult days ahead of you. he put everything in you for victory when he formed you in your mother's womb. So, arise! What He's done before has come for you!

WOMAN OF GOD "YOU ARE ELEGANT"

Respect creates elegance. Women who show the attitude of respect for others drench themselves in the sphere of elegance. Elegance, by definition, is refinement, grace, beauty in movement, appearance, or manners. Beauty in movement, as I see it, is your *gifting* and staying in your God-ordained lane as you do what God has graced you to do with this precious life of yours. Your refinement came because of your continuous getting up after falling. Now, you're able to say, "I am what I am by the grace of God."

WOMAN OF GOD "THERE IS NO DISCONNECT"

The Lord says, "I am removing this emotional fog the enemy has brought to surround you with as he tries to cause a disconnect between you and My plans for your life. There is no disconnect between you and My purpose. For as you praise Me this day, it will cause the fog to lift and you will know that My glory has prevailed in your life."

WOMAN OF GOD "YOU ARE FIRST"

Hear what the Spirit of the LORD is saying to you: "But many who are first will be last, and the last first." Many women run their families by themselves, but the Lord is saying, "I am shifting you now into the lead. No longer will you be last—last to get this, last to get that. For I am making you first in all things. Your assignment from Heaven is to live with no regret. I am moving in you mightily from this day!"

WOMAN OF GOD "YOU ARE UNIQUE"

God has made you unique—there's no one on earth like you. You were created by the glory/splendor of God to shine everywhere you go. God accepted you before you knew of yourself and being alive secures your position. Rise and move forward from your position of strength and get God's best that He has preserved for you. You are the glory of God!

WOMAN OF GOD "WALK BY FAITH"

The Lord says to you, "When I look at you, I see the brilliance I created in you. Oh, if you would just believe I'm for you in whatever you decide to do! I am here to empower, exceed, elevate, and excel you into excellence. Please Me by walking by faith and not by sight. I have you, my daughter, and I will never leave you, nor forsake you." Woman of God, release fear because excellence awaits your arrival!

WOMAN OF GOD "LET GO AND LET GOD"

Can you give up what you have worked hard for, prayed for, paid for, and dreamed? Can you leave these things behind for what and where God wants to take you, which is far better? If so, the answer to *Why are things getting so hard for me?* is LET GO AND LET GOD! Remember, His ways are higher than what you have worked hard for, prayed for, paid for, dreamed for, and are leaving. I'll see you at the Top where you belong!

WOMAN OF GOD "I AM YOUR DEVELOPER"

When you find yourself in the dark of not knowing what to do, God is there with you. He is your Developer. The picture/image/vision of you and your life will become clear. I know you are ready to come out, but He will not allow you to be underdeveloped. God will reveal the glory of the Lord in and through you.

WOMAN OF GOD "WALK TO YOUR VICTORY"

Don't allow the shadows of defeat to intimidate you to fear. They are just shadows that can't stop you from the victory that's already won by Christ Jesus on your behalf. Those shadows can't hurt you; they only make you hurt yourself. Get up and walk through them to your victory! I see you headed to the Top where you belong!

<u>WOMAN OF GOD "KEEP DREAMING"</u>

Keep the dream alive that God has shown you. Pick it back up and wear it as you would your sweater on a cool Autumn day. Your God-given dream will keep you warm while adding color when life appears dreary and gray. Yes, the dream will come to pass, and it will come to last.

WOMAN OF GOD "ACCELERATION IS YOUR PORTION"

The turbulent ride is over! Your life ahead is smoother with fewer trials. You will experience acceleration by the Spirit of God to make up for lost time, so you will be on time. What you learned is priceless for your destiny. Open doors await your arrival. You will now feel the winds behind you pushing you forward! Relax as you soar to your destination!

WOMAN OF GOD "RISE ABOVE LOW-GRADE THINKING"

There are times of the year where a heavy cloud of depression lingers in the atmosphere causing our minds to shift into low-grade thinking. In this depressive state of thinking, one can't seem to rise above the questions: *Why am I all alone? Why am I not further along? How come I'm not smart enough to make my life work? How come I'm always broke?*

Please understand, Woman of God, that God gives you the power to rise above low-grade thinking through the Holy Spirit who lives in you. What you need is a spiritual alignment. That spiritual alignment comes through the Word of God. There's a powerful word in the new testament—PARALAMBANO—to receive, to take, and to become the same with.

When you 'become the same with' what the Word says about you, you soar above low-grade thinking. Only then will you find the sun is shining bright where your mind now can tap into the possibilities that are exceedingly above all that you ask or think, according to the power that's working in you! Believe and become PARALAMBANO—the same with what God says about you. I see you at the Top rising above the depression where you belong!

WOMAN OF GOD "FINISH STRONG"

You will need to finish strong in these next few months, so you will have the momentum to do the extraordinary things God is calling you to do. You've asked Him to work great things in and through you. Well, God has answered your requests. This new thing is bigger than you and will take the wisdom of God and faith to move mountains.

God desires to show Himself strong through you with a global influence. Step outside of the normal because He has granted you favor and honor. Go for it. Don't look back but keep your eyes forward. God has completed your infrastructure through your past struggles! You're ready now to soar into destiny. This will be an unforgettable year of out of this world achievements! I'll know where to find you, that's at the Top where you belong!

WOMAN OF GOD "DON'T BACK DOWN"

No longer be intimated by what others may think of the title/office which God has called/ordained you. You have allowed the voices and stares of people to cause you to back down from taking ahold of that which God has spoken concerning *what* you are. God's voice is the divine voice above all voices. His voice is of absolute truth and total supreme authority.

Woman of God, you must align your voice with the voice of God concerning *what* you are. The Apostle Paul finally got it. In 1st Corinthians 15:10 (NKJV) he wrote, **"But by the grace of God I am what I am, and his grace toward me was not in**

vain; but I labored more abundantly than they all, yet not I, but the grace of God which was with me." So, His grace called you to *what* you are.

In Jeremiah 1:5 (NKJV), God said, **"Before I formed you in the womb I knew you; before you were born I sanctified you; I ordained you a prophet to the nations."** If He ordained you an Apostle, Prophet, Evangelist, Pastor, Teacher, etc., walk in it. Never be ashamed of the title that may come with it! If He called you to be a Bishop, stay in it even if the world refutes it because their voice didn't command, "Let there be light." Woman of God, walk it out! And in the Power of His might, I now release Apostolic impartation upon you to be *what* you are! I'll see you at the Top where you belong!

WOMAN OF GOD "DIVINE ELEVATION IS YOURS"

You have entered a season of divine elevation. Think it not strange that God has ordered your flight into elevated places of authority and great influences. Certain moves of a God won't take place until you get there because the miraculous will come through the words of your mouth. Healing and comfort will come from your touch because God has anointed you for such a time as this. Your 'Yes Lord' will bless a multitude of people and yourself. Get your passport business in order, so you can go when He opens the doors to the world. He will become the air you breathe at this new height of elevation. Take it all in and soar letting nothing from your past ground you. Favor surrounds you! I'll see you at the Top where you belong!

WOMAN OF GOD "YOU HAVE A PLACE AT THE TOP"

You may feel your life is an uphill climb to the bottom. Woman of God, you can't get so low that God can't lift you. His grace is miraculous; His love is depthless; and His power is endless. Dare to believe because He wants to walk with you to the finish line. I know you're in an uphill climb to the bottom, but He wants to walk with you to the Top where you belong!

WOMAN OF GOD "THERE IS GREATER"

Everything is coming greater than before. You have a GREATER to proclaim, a GREATER to possess, a GREATER anointing, a GREATER faith, a GREATER peace, a GREATER wisdom, a GREATER joy, a GREATER to stand in, a GREATER to receive, a GREATER to walk in, a GREATER song to sing, a GREATER platform to operate from, a GREATER level of loving, a GREATER health report, a GREATER financial position, a GREATER ministry, and a GREATER YOU! I will see you at the Top where you belong!

WOMAN OF GOD "ALTITUDE OF GREATNESS"

So often you've allowed the beggarly elements of the traditions of man to keep you from soaring to the altitude of greatness God has reserved for you to climb. I decree your freedom that cut those ties that has held you down, and I now declare that you are free to climb to your God- ordained altitude of greatness in Him. I will see you at the Top where you belong!

WOMAN OF GOD "YOU WILL LAND ON YOUR FEET"

Although you may feel your life is in a free fall, nonetheless, God is still in control and has ordered your steps. You will land upright on your feet at the appointed place! Fear not, for He is with you, and will never leave you! He's putting you in new circles with power. The leader in you will emerge. I'll see you at the Top where you belong!

WOMAN OF GOD "START OVER"

Starting over after any loss is debilitating. Your whole life seems turned upside down. Your equilibrium is off, causing you to live your life in an off-balance state. But God has given you the Holy Spirit Who will bring you back into harmony. The Holy Spirit will more than make up the difference despite what you lost in your life. He is the Way Maker from loss to life, from wrong to right, from condemnation to celebration, from fear to faith, and from ashes to beauty. You will recover love and life, and you will laugh again! From the bottom to the Top where you belong!

WOMAN OF GOD "IT'S ALREADY ALRIGHT!"

The Spirit of God told me to tell you, "It's all right!" So, make the move; He's already gone before you. It will not take a miracle, but it will take a leap of faith on your part. God has set everything in place upon your arrival. No small steps, but a GIANT leap. It's already all right because the joy of the LORD is your strength! To the Top you go where you belong!

WOMAN OF GOD "SOMETHING ABOUT THAT WOMAN"

You are original, exceptional, effectual, and essential. With every loss there comes pain, but you will also experience gain. If you don't close your eyes, you will see the gain of wisdom. She will be your insight into the better developed you. Is there something about that Woman, or is there something about YOU, woman? I see you going to the Top where you belong!

WOMAN OF GOD "STAY FOCUSED"

Learn to focus until it comes into focus. When the voices or sounds come, don't let it distract you from the object of your focus. After it comes into focus, just keep moving forward until you possess it. I'll see you at the Top where you belong!

PART II

"BIRD DROPPINGS ARE NOT FOR YOU"

WOMAN OF GOD "THERE'S AN ANOINTING ON YOUR LIFE"

Your friendships have been the womb to conceive many people's dreams simply by your words of kindness, encouragement, and your nurturing spirit. You may never know it on this side of Heaven the people you have helped, but by encountering you, it was the anointing on your life that brought out the blessings of the Lord in the lives of others. You were not a causal 'bump into' but was divinely placed by God to impart life through the Life of Jesus Christ. And just like Mary, the Mother of Jesus, the Holy Spirit is your only source.

WOMAN OF GOD "YOUR LIFE IS NOT OVER"

Do you think God would have His plans for your life wrapped up in a man who rejected you, walked out on you, betrayed you, and mistreated your love? And now you think your life is over? One and done? Not even possible! God already knew, so He saved your best for now. Woman of God, rise from your despair and wipe away your tears. A brighter sunshine awaits your rising. Take ahold of the new, greater possibilities that God has placed before you. Dare to receive all that God has revealed can be yours for the taking. You got this! I'll see you at the Top where you belong!

WOMAN OF GOD "YOU ARE FEARFULLY AND WONDERFULLY MADE"

Don't allow flattery, lies, or your need for a stimulus to cross your emotional wires. You are *fearfully* and *wonderfully* made. A person that is God-sent will speak words of life that will add to your being; not words of counterfeit that will bankrupt you emotionally. Keep yourself together, and I will see you at the Top where you rightfully belong!

WOMAN OF GOD "WHY?

Why do you keep going back to where God has delivered you? Did you forget about the verbal, mental, and physical abuse? Don't those times count? Don't you deserve treatment better than that? Isn't life more than wishing happiness from someone who can't give happiness to you? Don't you have the need for respect? Get out and don't look back. God's absolute best awaits your coming out.

WOMAN OF GOD "A MOMENT OF TIME"

The enemy tries to get you to mess your life up 'in a moment of time' by deciding what people, places, and things are not a part of your kingdom destiny! Understand God is never apart from you in those 'moments of time'. Don't get tripped up by what looks good, sounds good, and feels good. Everything that looks good is not God! Stay on track; don't set your life back. Your destiny is at stake. If you are off track, I hear the LORD saying, "There's a U-turn just ahead for you!" I will see you at the Top!

WOMAN OF GOD "IT'S NOT YOUR FAULT"

Many men have accused you of mishandling their emotions, but the truth is they have mishandled their own emotions by expecting you to be the sole provider of their emotions. You're called to be a helpmate to your husband in every area of his life. Thus, the two of you becoming one successful whole union. God has equipped you with wisdom and grace to bring out of him what he couldn't on his own. But he must be willing to self-reflect and go from sitting and waiting to standing and moving. He must lead you somewhere positive. If not, the relationship will become stagnant and an implosion will occur.

WOMAN OF A GOD "YOU'RE NO HANDOUT"

You're not a handout to someone who's needy. You're favor to someone who God was adding to his life when He added you to them. So, don't allow someone to treat you as a handout. When a man finds a wife, he finds a *good* thing that God has done in her, and it adds favor unto that man. Even if you're not yet married or are divorced, He has still done a good thing in you. You're still the 'favor factor' wherever God sends you—to church, work, or amongst people—if God has added you to them, you're not a handout, but you are favor from God to them. God created you to be celebrated. Now go to the Top where you belong because you are the FAVOR sent from God!

WOMAN OF GOD "BIRD DROPPINGS ARE NOT FOR YOU!"

I want to appeal to the hearts of my daughters—spiritual, biological, and daughters of the hurting parents, aunts, grandparents, uncles, sisters, and brothers who have accepted a life of bird droppings from men who have nothing to offer them that will help in making their lives work for the glory of God. I'm not speaking of the God-fearing men who are doing what's right in the sight of God—speaking life to the women that God has brought into their lives. I applaud those men who take care of their women in the fear and respect of their God.

All of us know men who are nothing but selfish, controlling, vicious, irresponsible, angry, and lifeless—men with no heart for the future good of their woman or children. To the daughters everywhere, I ask you: Why have you chosen, as an act of your free will, to hook up with, have children with, stay with, suffer under, and accept bird droppings from these kinds of men? Most of you didn't get tricked into being with him. There were many, many signs along the way that read: **Danger, Stay Away From**. What caused you to ignore the warnings and the voices of your loved ones? How has your conscious become so seared that you found the basis of your foundation on sinking sand?

Love? What is there to love? Why is your standard of love reduced to smacks, insults, outside relationships, etc.? What's keeping you from hearing and receiving the truth which is the beginning of freedom? I'm asking you these questions to perk your thinking. God has a strategy and plan for you called 'Launch out into the deep'. But your faith must be in Him and His Word to make this work for you. Your mind must be made up as to no turning around or going back!

I'm not here to say it will be easy. But how bad do you want it? Now is the time! Jesus has given you power (authority) over every unclean spirit. The Father, God, has given you the power of the Holy Spirit to do the impossible. Just ask and receive right now and God will endow you with this greatness to make your life work for you and yours! God will connect you along the way with people who will help you. Bird droppings are no longer your portion; you have a glorious future and a hope. Let God take you from *Nowhere to Everywhere*. I'll meet you at the Top where you belong!

WOMAN OF GOD "LET HIM BUY HIS OWN SET OF NEW TIRES!"

There are seasons where smiles become warmer and much needed because of the cold weather. During this time of year, hearts grow fonder, and we often love making loved ones and friends glow with gifts from our hearts to let them know they're on our minds. But it's also the time of year when predators roam—exes manipulate with false kindness vying for your generosity. Warning daughters: **keep your money and your heart on alert**! Don't even play with the small talk; you'll look and feel foolish without nothing to show for it (again).

Spend your time with those who celebrate you, not tolerate you until the season of giving. Those who celebrate you feel content with being around you without it costing you. Those who tolerate you want you to *pay* to *play*. Don't give your money away; don't even lend it away. Keep your money. Go into this year and all the following years on Top where you belong!

YOUNG WOMAN OF GOD "USE YOUR HEAD TO PROTECT YOUR HEART"

I once read an article that said there are more first-time mothers than married first-time mothers. It talked about the hardships that come with having a child or children outside of marriage. For these women, there are usually years of struggling financially, getting a subpar education, and having to go on public assistance for years. There are exceptions where that doesn't have to happen to first-time unmarried mothers, but it's the norm—the struggling and all that comes with it. I want to praise all the young ladies who have made it work for them and their children, but I also want to speak to young ladies before they get out there and let themselves get pregnant by someone who is not marriage material—all talk but little substance.

Young woman of God, you need to protect yourself and your life by getting and keeping yourself together. Don't think every young man wants to marry you. Some only want to sleep with you then scamper away leaving you fighting for child support while you're rocking a child alone. So, use your head to protect your heart. Think things through before getting emotionally wrapped up with an irresponsible, smooth-talking young man who can't see past his sexual desires. Yes, he will get it from someone else if you don't give yourself to him for pleasure, but he wasn't the one God has out there for you if he does that.

Be patient and wait on God to send you a husband no matter how long it takes. It may take years and more years, but God has a process. He's working on you and your future husband, so let God finish His work, then your husband will find you.

The Bible declares in Proverbs 18:22 (NKJV), **"He who finds a wife finds a good thing."**

Woman of God, you won't be a *thing*, but God is doing a good thing in you that will make you a wonderful wife. Don't come cheap by giving yourself away to just anyone. Why does God have to show you so many signs for you to know if that young man deserves you or not when the young man shows you that he's not the one by how he talks to you, treats you, and disrespects you and your feelings? Those are signs. Be strong, get your life on course, get on the right track, and take life with God to the Top of the mountain where you belong!

WOMAN OF GOD "DON'T ACCEPT MINIMUM HAPPINESS"

Because you're a nurturer, you fed into the man who's in your life. As you continue to nurture him, you became more and more attached to him emotionally despite his behavior. Even though there are signs that he's using you and your kindness, you keep getting in deeper, hoping that your actions will change his attitude towards you.

You must understand it doesn't take much from a man to receive from you because he knows it makes you feel good to show your love for him— even if he's only dropping you off minimum happiness or his time. You will always be only an *option* in his life, and a man who is not righteous can have many options at one time in his life because he's not giving but only receiving emotionally.

You must break from this cycle of emotional deceit. God has allowed you to see the signs, but you keep ignoring those signs by justifying them through your tainted desires that it will change if you just hang in there. Woman of God, God has opened your eyes to see what's in front of you, so He can give you the strength to move on with wisdom and the capacity to carry His glory that will make your life prosperous. Stop reading the same old pages of the same book of your life. Turn the page. There are exciting things in store for you in the following chapters of your life. I'll see you at the Top where you belong!

WOMAN OF GOD "HEAD TOWARD THE TOP!"

Being in pursuit of a relationship that has gone south may cause you to lower your standards. Stop, turn around, and head towards the top where your standards will cause you to feel better about yourself. It starts in your mind. And whoever or whatever has your mind, has you. Take your mind back so you can use your mind to guard your heart. I hear the prize of the High calling. It's calling you to the Top in Jesus' name!

WOMAN OF GOD "HE HAS MADE YOU COMPLEX NOT COMPLICATED"

When people want to control you or change you, they label you 'complicated'. But you are fearfully and wonderfully made by God in His image. The pain you feel is the layers being stripped off you by the actions of others. But not anymore! You can and will stop this right now as God is restoring you to new! I see you headed to the Top!

WOMAN OF GOD "YOU ARE GOOD ENOUGH"

If you are good enough for bed, aren't you good enough to wed? If you are good enough to lie down with, aren't you good enough to walk down the aisle? If you are good enough to understand, aren't you good enough to become the wife of that man? Woman of God, Heaven doesn't want you having any regrets. Take yourself to the Top where you belong!

WOMAN OF GOD "TRICKS ARE FOR KIDS"

No matter how sweet it seems, sounds, or presents itself, a lie is still a lie! If it sounds like a duck and looks like a duck, Woman of God, it's a Duckling, and it can't fly that long to keep you! Right now, God is fixing it, so you can get your own, on your OWN! I will see you at the Top!

WOMAN OF GOD "DO NOT BE DISCOURAGED"

No longer feel discouraged in not having a husband *yet*. For the elevation that God is taking you, by His Spirit, will require the same of your future mate. This next Mighty move of God in your life is about ELEVATION in Him! You are going to the Top where you belong!

WOMAN OF GOD "REMOVE THE HEADACHE"

There are people in your life who come to *help* and some who come to bring you headaches. Don't get upset when the headache wants to leave! Understand God is removing the headache from your life to bring healing to your life. Now, you can celebrate, where in the past you used to tolerate! Turn your tears into cheers! I will see you at the Top!

WOMAN OF GOD "PUT YOUR HOPE IN CHRIST"

May your hope be in Christ and no one else. Hope *in*, before hoping *for*. If your hope is in a person, what you hope for may *feel* good to you but not *be* good for you. But hoping in Christ will assure what you hope for will be good for you because the source is in Christ. Many lives are messed up because their hope was in someone who could not be what they were hoping for. Christ in you is the hope of glory! I'll see you at the Top!

WOMAN OF GOD "IS IT WORTH IT?"

After the tears, fears, and finding yourself with yourself, the question becomes: *Is it worth it?* Is it worth delaying—if not giving up—your destiny? Is it worth pursuing what is supposed to be love, but is nothing but pain, heartbreak, anguish, and fear? You can't get to the Top that way. But today is a new *day* for a new *way*!

WOMAN OF GOD "YOU ALREADY HAVE A HEARTBEAT"

The Lord must remain the heartbeat of your life. Did He not say that He has come that you might have life, and that life more abundantly? So why do you try to make others and situations your heartbeat? Turn back to God, so He can guide you to your best life in Him. For He has a future of hope reserved for you.

WOMAN OF GOD "LIGHTEN YOUR LOAD"

The Lord is saying to you, "Lighten the load." I would like to encourage you to spend this weekend cutting loose that which no longer is worth your time, tears, and trouble. For every person you cut away, God will match it in the unknown parts of your spirit. By Sunday's end, you will be praising Him at a new level! You will walk in a new sense of authority, and your health will be complete from dropping all the excess.

WOMAN OF GOD "DON'T DISQUALIFY YOURSELF"

I'm not an advocate for dating younger men, but I feel that God appoints men and women for relationships leading to marriage. Too many women miss God's appointment as it relates to *"when a man finds a wife, he finds a good thing"* because they disqualify themselves by not allowing themselves to date younger available men of God appointed by God and positioned by God to find you.

The youngest King in the Bible, Jehoash, was only seven-years-old. Maybe your King will be years younger than you, but he will be appointed by God. He will be a Godly man, and not seven-years-old, nor under the age of marriage, but he will be sent by God! Don't allow what people may say and how they may feel keep you from the happiness that God has planned for your life. If he's sent by God, he will love you and your children.

WOMAN OF GOD, "YOU ARE A QUEEN SELECTED"

A Queen *elected* is not yet a Queen *selected*, but both know a King when they see one! God has made them both elected, but the King makes her, by marriage, a Queen selected. An elected Queen is one who is still in the making—the one who God is doing that 'good thing' in her, so she is found by her King. Woman of God, you may experience many lonely nights, but He is doing in you a 'good thing'. You may be years learning to walk independently while watching your friends become taken in marriage, but He is doing a 'good thing' in you.

You may have given into lust a time or two and had children out of wedlock raising them by yourself, yet He is still doing a 'good things' in you. You may pinch pennies, rob Peter to pay Paul, tell a few lies to get by, but He is STILL doing a 'good things' in you. Love may have tricked you, lied to you, abused you, used you, shamed you, and left you to die, but Queen elected, you are still here because according to Philippians 1:6 (NKJV), **"He who has begun a good work in you will complete it..."**

Your selection is coming by a God appointed King who will love you, honor you, protect you, and take Godly care of you. Stay *elected* until *selected* because you're a Queen! You can still own your own business, buy yourself a fancy car, buy yourself a beautiful home, go to France, wear what you like, and be *what* you are by His grace! I will see you at the Top where you belong!

WOMAN OF GOD "OPEN YOUR SPIRITUAL EYES"

In 1st Samuel 16:7 (NKJV), the Lord said to Samuel, **"Do not look at his appearance or at his physical stature, because I have refused him."** Woman of God, the LORD does not see as (wo)man sees. For (wo)man looks at the outward appearance, but the LORD looks at the heart. The man who God has for you has an anointed heart to love you.

WOMAN OF GOD "PAY ATTENTION TO WHAT YOU SEE"

The Lord never said, "You will know them by their words spoken to you." But He said, "You shall know them by their fruit." It's not what you hear, but what you see. Walking by faith and not by sight is your connection to God, but with people, it's their fruit that shows who they are. With man, nothing from nothing will always leave you with nothing. But God knows how to take nothing and make something. Ask yourself, "Where's the fruit?"

WOMAN OF GOD "DON'T LOSE YOURSELF"

Don't lose yourself trying to hang on to someone who doesn't value your worth. If you lose yourself, you have dropped the value of your worth to that person and to yourself. Your life is meant to be celebrated, not tolerated. Do YOU all the way to the Top!

WOMAN OF GOD "DO WHAT GOD HAS TOLD YOU"

Sometimes God will harden the hearts of the people He's trying to get you to leave like He did to Pharaoh. In Exodus 10:20 (NKJV) it reads, **"But the LORD hardened Pharaoh's heart, and he (Pharaoh) did not let the children of Israel go."** Often, if they treat us good, we stay even though God told us to leave, so He allowed them to treat us bad so it would drive us to leave! Woman of God, do what God has told you to do and leave the consequences of your obeying up to Him! NO REGRETS!

WOMAN OF GOD "CHECK HIS TRACK RECORD"

Check the track record of your ex as to how he has taken care of his children in the past. Now, why did you believe he would get your children's school clothing and school supplies? You're feeling bad right now because you haven't taken the trash from the garage of your heart. I'm not calling your children's Father 'trash', but the effects of his ways, as it relates to you and your children, are trash. Take it out! I declare that your God shall supply your needs according to His riches and glory by Christ Jesus. Now go put it on the curb so God can put into the heart of your garage His treasure to replace the trash. I see you exhaling now. It's okay to praise Him out loud. You're going to the Top in no time!

WOMAN OF GOD "DON'T EXCHANGE LOVE FOR PAIN"

When contemplating getting into a love relationship, be careful when giving your heart/love away. If you see you will exchange your love for pain, don't do it. You can read the signs that are posted, but you can't change what's written on the sign that reads: *Warning, this will cause you nothing but Pain.* Woman of God, use your head/wisdom to protect your heart because the value of your love is of a premium/superior quality. Love thyself to protect thyself!

WOMAN OF GOD "DON'T FALL FOR EXCUSES"

Why would you and how could you date or marry a man you know for certain does not pay child support? The money he's trying to impress you with is not his but belongs to his children. What excuses has he given you as to why he doesn't pay child support anymore that you have fallen for? He probably says, "She spends the money on herself...All she does is spend it on her new boyfriend...She won't let me see the kids...Her mother takes care of the kids more than she does..."

Woman of God, there is no excuse for a man not to pay child support for the support of his children! He may be a nice guy to you, but he's not being a supportive guy to his children. His heart is not right towards his children, so how can his heart be right towards you? God forbid if you have a child with him and the two of you don't make it together. Well, at least you'll know how the other women feel.

There's something rotten about a man who won't pay child support! And when you knowingly allow him to feel good about being with you, then you're a part of the rottenness that's being served to his children. I know what it is to pay child support. My first wife and I have four children. When we couldn't make it together anymore (thank God for second chances), NOBODY had to make me take care of my children (no applause please) because it was the only thing to do! Before we went to court, I was paying child support to my soon-to-be ex-wife not because of the court order, but because they were my children. Today, they are grown. All I'm trying to say is don't be part of the problem! It's a matter of character. I'll see you at the Top where you belong!

WOMAN OF GOD "GET IN PROPER ALIGNMENT"

It's a terrible thing to have your own heart deceive you into falling in love when love was not even a choice. Now that you know *what* happened, the next step is to find out *why* it happened; then, how it happened. Woman of God, gather up the fragmented pieces of your heart and take it to the LORD so He can repair it and put it in proper alignment. And remember, no matter what the fallout may be, His grace suffices to carry you from here to there. I'll see you at the Top where you belong.

WOMAN OF GOD "MR. RIGHT OR MR. RIGHT NOW"

There's a big difference in *Mr. Right* and *Mr. Right Now*! Mr. Right will be for you, looking out for your best interest until death do you apart. But with Mr. Right Now, you will cater everything to his convenience. *Now* is his last name, so even when you're being pressured in a situation that you're not mentally ready for, Mr. Right Now wants what he wants *Right Now*!

You dated Mr. Right Now, and you got pregnant and left to raise the child by yourself even though you didn't get pregnant by yourself. But when you wait on Mr. Right, his mentality is to meet your every need—your need for respect, love, appreciation, consideration, and good, life-building conversation. Mr. Right carries these qualifications all the days of his life for you. So, take another look and decide which one it will be because you have a choice in the matter. Will it be *Mr. Right* or *Mr. Right Now*? I'll meet you at the Top where you and *Mr. Right* belong!

WOMAN OF GOD "BRUTE OR DOORMAT"

When love is over and gone, you might discover that you built it wrong. Don't use the same materials of low self-esteem, fear, loneliness, unforgiveness, sex, and desperation to build with again. Then, you will have to become either a brute or a doormat to keep him, which neither is any good. Develop and use the fruits of the Spirit led by the Holy Spirit! I'll see you at the Top where you belong!

WOMAN OF GOD "IT'S NOT WHAT YOU SAW..."

One reason your relationships are not working is because an illusion deceived you. Although the illusion portrays everything will work perfectly in the relationship, the real thing never adds up to the illusion. Today is the day to snap out of it and wake up. It is what it is, and you need to decide if you will stay or if you will go based on what's real and what's not real. You are too gifted to be riding in the back seat of your life. It's time you drive in the direction that will make your life work! Turn right and follow the sign that reads: **To the Top where you belong**! I will see you there!

WOMAN OF GOD "NO MORE DANCING IN THE DARK"

It's time for you to take center stage. No one is holding you back more than you are. You keep giving yourself away for known broken promises. No more dancing in the dark with him who doesn't want to be seen with just you. Your stage is awaiting you. The lights have been lit up just for you on the platform with your name on it! The sound of applauds are in anticipation of your arrival from nowhere, to somewhere, then on to everywhere! That God-given gift in you empowers people all over the world. No more dancing in the dark. You can see the light at the Top where you belong!

WOMAN OF GOD "FROM EX TO EXCELLENCE"

Memories of past relationships often can have a halting effect that keeps you from moving freely into the future that God has for you. The word 'ex' means without or excluding. He's your 'ex' because he excluded something from the relationship that you needed. You went without in the relationship; therefore, creating the 'ex' position where you now stand. Now, the memories are halting your moving on to the better that's in front of you, but you must cast those thoughts of yesteryear and yesterday and move toward the new possibilities that await you. Cut the cords that keep you tied to going nowhere! Your light shows you the things that are before you. Walk by faith, and not by memories. Turn your life from 'ex' to excellence! I'll see you at the Top where you belong!

WOMAN OF GOD "POWER HAS ARRIVED"

Strong ankle bones are a necessity for jumping to your feet or for pivoting around and getting out of unfavorable situations. As it relates to relationships, you may have strong feet or strong legs, but if you don't have strong ankles bones, you will sit there amidst the turbulence carried from one trouble to the next trouble by the one who's causing you to rock back and forth, going nowhere.

I declare, through faith in His name, that power comes to your ankle bones, so you will jump to your feet in the name of Jesus and run, leap, and soar above that turbulent, decayed, and dead relationship! Run to the hills of God where you will rest from weariness. A refreshing awaits you as you jump, leap, and soar your way to the Top where you belong!

WOMAN OF GOD "MOVE ON"

Letting go of someone who you've had emotional ties with can be a hard thing to do when they have been a source of your happiness at some point. They have also been the reason for your tears, unhappiness, emotional pains, and mental sufferings. Your pattern has been let go, take back, let go, take back, let go again, and take back again. You keep repeating this cycle. All the while, your self-esteem is becoming lower and lower until happiness with this person is just an illusion of what once was neither fulfilling nor substantial.

Now, you don't like yourself because of the way you've allowed yourself to be used like a ping-pong ball being battered between no-good decisions. Woman of God, it's time to move forward. Moving on is a decision that starts in the mind. Today is 'Move on Day'. Decide to move towards the greater for yourself. God will give you the strength, wisdom, and direction you will need to make your life work for you. Decide not to go back. Instead, move forward! I'll see you at the Top where you belong!

WOMAN OF GOD "STOP SELLING YOURSELF SHORT"

God did not make you to be a discount, so stop short-changing yourself to get the approval of a man. When you sell yourself short, you're displaying that you aren't worthy of your full value. So, you come at a discount to someone who will not respect you, anyway! You must love yourself enough to value your God-given worth. If he can't respect your worth, he is not worthy of you, anyway.

Why give yourself to someone who can't afford to, or doesn't have enough in them to respect the whole you? So, he hides you away, buried under piles of 'you're not enough for me' actions. The

159

truth is you're too much for him to handle! Maybe he knows he does not handle, love, speak words of life to, and show outward affection to someone with your value. Woman of God, you're worth more than the rarest of rubies. You are the blessing someone needs and wants to love and show appreciation to! Once you calculate your worth, I'll see you at the Top where you belong!

WOMAN OF GOD "DON'T FALL IN LOVE BEFORE YOUR TIME"

Love is the strongest emotion you have, but you must protect it, so it doesn't fall into the hands of someone who only seeks to shatter it into many pieces. Don't fall in love before it's time. Lay the groundwork before putting your heart on an unpaved road to nowhere but hurt and pain at the hands of someone you knew didn't qualify for your love in the first place. Stop the madness, break the cycle of the same pattern, and go in a new direction. Don't give up on love. Just be more cautious where placing your love. If he is in love with you, then he will do the work to prove it. If the work only causes you pain, then do the work to take your heart back out of love for yourself. I'll see you at the Top where you belong!

WOMAN OF GOD "AND THE BEATS GO'S ON"

Like a heart that beats before it's fully formed, so is the essence of you. In your last relationship, you found out you were not fully formed. The relationship knocked you down but not out. And every time life knocked you down, you got back up stronger. Not only have you learned to make the melody you dance to, but now you're writing the song that steer your chart-topping life. You have taken over the helm of your life and have become the producer of your life's story. You have created your own beat and style and will no longer kiss frogs or allow dogs to chase you. God will provide the sound of rain, you will discover your personal rainbow, and life will become more abundant. I'll see you at the Top where you belong!

WOMAN OF GOD "DON'T GET HELD UP"

How many times have your desire for a man to hold you turned into you, your dreams, and your esteem being held captive by that same man? It's okay to want to be held, but it's not okay to hold yourself up by being controlled by someone who has taken control of your mind. Your mind is very important to maintain. It's your creativity source that makes you the unique person you are. Be free to be yourself—creative, confidant, and capable of achieving all that your destiny requires of you! I'll see you at the Top where you belong!

WOMAN OF GOD "IT IS WHAT IT IS..."

When the love is gone, it's gone. There's no further reason to stay a statue when all that makes you live and move is taken out of you. Every day you cry, and every day is a rainy day, so why stay? You've felt heartbreak time and time again, and it seems there will be no end. But your God has a future and hope for you. Yes, He has a plan that may or may not involve another man. God created you for more than this hurt and what you're going through in this moment. You can see by his actions he has nothing for you. So, rise from there—out of that despair—knowing the God who's inside of you is calling you to a new spot that will take you to the Top!

WOMAN OF GOD "MAKE SURE"

When sharing your mind with a man, make sure he can handle the depths that make up who you are. Make sure he knows you're more than the skirt you wear or the pants that hug your curves. There's much more to you than flesh; there's the blood of Jesus that empowers you toward greatness.

You're not just the style of your hair. Your heart cares to be all God has whispered in your ear that you could be. You are much more than something to play with then throw aside. Make sure he can cheer you on, push you gently, and hold you steady while whispering in your ear, "You will make it to the Top where you belong."

WOMAN OF GOD "NO GAP FILLER"

No man can effectively love two women at the same time, but he can hurt and ruin two women's lives. Make the decision that if he's in between relationships, you will not be the one he uses to fill in the gap. A piece of man is NOT better than having no man at all. You're not a *piece* of a woman; you're a *whole* woman who deserves a *whole* man. You serve a whole God who will only give you a whole man. You may have been broken pieces at one time in your life, but God has put you back together better than ever and more secure and smarter than ever. I'll meet you at the Top where you belong!

WOMAN OF GOD "STAY BALANCED"

Don't get swept off your feet by the sweetness and sensitivity of a kind man. When you're 'swept' off your feet, you can become unbalanced in a few of your once stable ways. The compromising of strong beliefs is breached because of the flood of emotions the sweet sensitivity produced. Keep your balance, so you won't succumb to your emotions. To make it plain, because you are a giver of life and love, sweet sensitivity soon becomes sex.

Yes, he is sweet and displays sensitivity in his kindness towards you but be careful that you don't allow your feelings to run out of bounds. Thus, disqualifying the good that God has done within you, and that He has yet to do in your life. Deeds—whether good or bad—follow feelings. When feelings are out of bounds, reasoning becomes blurred, and you do what you never thought you would do. But you wouldn't if you knew that you were out of bounds with uncontrolled feelings.

Woman of God, now is the time to turn to the keeper of your soul and say to Him, "Sit on me and my feelings, Lord, until it's safe to turn me loose. Your way, not my way, in Jesus name. Amen." I'll see you at the Top where you belong!

WOMAN OF GOD "YOU ARE MORE THAN ENOUGH"

When someone walks out of your life, those feelings of defeat come from you feeling you were not enough to keep them from leaving. But often that's not the case. It was them not being enough within themselves that caused that person to leave searching for something else, not understanding that what they are searching for will never appear because the deficiency lies in them.

You were more than enough without being too much. So, wipe away your tears, get up from where you are, take in the grace of God, and move in the power of the Holy Spirit—toward a new abundant life that God still has waiting for you. You will not only get through this, but you will flourish into the brilliant butterfly you are. I'll meet you at the Top where you belong!

WOMAN OF GOD "DON'T GO THERE"

Sex with him, no matter how you serve it, will not make him want to marry you! Having his baby won't do it either. Yes, I call you a woman of God. Sometimes, we get caught up in emotions, and before you know it, we've found ourselves hooked into something trying to make it work—something that never had a chance at working in the first place. The Spirit of God told you not to go there—not to go into that situation—but you thought you knew something He didn't know about him, and that you could somehow change him with the way you do what you do. So, you dug yourself into a deeper hole.

Men love sports, and to some men, sex is nothing more than a recreational activity at the expense of your dreams. But God, who is rich in mercy, is extending His outreached hands to you to help you make the best of this situation. It's called reconciliation where He restores you back unto Himself if you will ask Him.

God's grace suffices to cover, restore, heal, and promote your life if you will come to Him and ask Him for His help with a renewed mind. Learn, so you can teach someone else how to keep themselves for the one God has for them. I want to see you at the Top where you really belong!

WOMAN OF GOD "YOU'RE THE BRIGHT SIDE OF HIM"

There are times when you must let him keep his own personal thoughts to himself, so he can mature them in the process of his thinking. Men who are always asked to reveal what they are thinking about may reveal thoughts that might be immature having not been fully developed yet. When these immature thoughts are revealed to you, it may cause confusion in the relationship. When you comment negatively to an undeveloped thought, it stops him from communicating with you.

Men are solution-driven thinkers and are easily frustrated by a woman who is more seasoned in her process of thinking which causes them to want to display their physicality towards women—trying to relate to the body and not the mind hoping this will give them an upper hand. Help him by adding well-placed words to his revealed thoughts, not cutting his words to pieces causing shame. You're the bright side of him. When you shine, he shines.

WOMAN OF GOD "DON'T BE THAT WOMAN"

Don't be the woman who every man wants, be the woman who one *right* man needs. He will see you, not because he needs you, but because you need him. Thus, all needs are being met. I will see you at the Top where you belong!

IN CLOSING...

With great expectations, I decree God's very best for your life from the moment you've read this until God translates you to Heaven. I declare God's favor over you and your household in the greatest measure possible until you take your last breath here on earth. It is through faith in His name, the name of Jesus, that I both decree and declare these great blessings over you and yours. Amen!

Apostle Lee Harris

ABOUT THE AUTHOR

Apostle Lee Harris lives in Memphis, TN with his wife, Apostle Davida Harris, by way of Compton, CA. In 1989, Apostle Harris become an ordained Minister. He then became a Bishop, and in 2011, he accepted his calling to Apostleship.

Apostle Harris and his wife have eight grown children and are Pastors of Dramatic Grace and Faith church in Memphis, TN and Word of Impact Global Ministries. Under Word of Impact Global Ministries, the pair travel the world internationally to spread love and the Word of God.

Made in the USA
Columbia, SC
04 December 2020